The STORYBOOK COLLECTION

MACDONALD YOUNG BOOKS

This edition first published in Great Britain in 1995 by
Macdonald Young Books Ltd
Campus 400
Maylands Avenue
Hemel Hempstead HP2 7EZ

Babybug first published in 1992 by
Simon & Schuster Young Books,
text © 1992 Catherine Storr,
illustrations © 1992 Fiona Dunbar

Mandy's Mermaid first published in 1993 by
Simon & Schuster Young Books,
text © 1993 Anne Forsyth,
illustrations © 1993 Thelma Lambert

Princess by Mistake first appeared in
Jubilee Jackanory, published by the BBC in 1977
and was then reprinted in **Uninvited Ghosts** published
by William Heinemann Ltd in 1984. Published as a
storybook by Simon & Schuster Young Books in 1993,
text © 1977 Penelope Lively,
illustrations © 1993 Julie Anderson

Mog and Bumble first published in 1991 by
Simon & Schuster Young Books,
text © 1991 Catherine Robinson,
illustrations © 1991 Alice Englander

Printed and bound in Portugal by Ediçoes ASA

ISBN 0 7500 1786 4

Contents

Catherine Storr

Illustrated by Fiona Dunbar

For Paul

Chapter 1

"What's that?" Tania asked.

"It's your old baby alarm," Dad said.

"What's it for?"

"If I plug this bit into the electric socket here in the kitchen, we can hear right through to our bedroom where the other half is," Dad said, and he plugged it in. "Listen," he said.

Tania listened. She couldn't hear anything.

"Adam must be asleep. You'd hear him all right if he was awake," Dad said.

Tania did not want to hear Adam. She was sick and tired of the baby.

Before he'd been born, she had quite looked forward to having a little brother or sister. This was what she'd been promised. She had imagined someone like young Simon down the road, who was five, or Sally, who was almost her own age and fun to play with. But when Adam was born, he turned out to be small and useless. He couldn't walk, he couldn't talk, he took up almost all of Mum's time and he cried a lot. Why should anyone want to hear him cry some more?

"So that if he needs me I can go and see to
him," Mum said.

"Can he hear us talking in here?" Tania
asked.

"No. The alarm only works one way. If we
wanted to be in the bedroom and listen to
what's going on in the kitchen, we'd have to
switch the plugs round," Dad said.

"Tania can't understand that," Mum said.

"Yes, she can. Tania's very good at
understanding how things work," Dad said,
and Tania was pleased. At least this was
something that boring little Adam couldn't do.

"Did you have that . . . baby alarm . . . for
me?" Tania asked.

"We bought it just before you were born.
It's seven years old. Hope it's still working,"
Dad said.

At that moment there was a squeaky sort of
wail from the baby alarm. "Mew . . . mew . . .
mew . . . aah!" it said.

"It's as good as ever," Dad said.

"I'll go," Mum said, and disappeared.

"Could you hear something quiet? A
whisper?" Tania asked.

"Listen now," Dad said, and Tania put her ear down near to the electric socket and she heard Mum's voice saying very softly, "There now! That's better, isn't it? What a little greedy!" And she could hear tiny snorts and grunts as the baby fed.

"I can hear everything!" she said.

"It's like what spies are supposed to use, so that they can hear people's secrets. They stick these things in walls and in telephones and then if anyone is plotting something bad, they know about it and stop it. Bugs, they're called when spies use them, but for babies they're called alarms," Dad said.

"I thought bugs were creepy-crawly things like we have in the garden," Tania said.

"That's one kind. This is another. But the kind spies use are much smaller so that they don't show. That's probably why they're called bugs," Dad said, and went into the kitchen to prepare the special supper he cooked for Mum and Tania every Saturday night.

Chapter 2

Tania went on thinking about bugs. She liked the idea of hearing other people's secrets. She thought she would listen to the alarm in the kitchen when Mum was talking to someone in her bedroom. That would be much more interesting than hearing Adam crying because he was hungry.

But she didn't always like what she heard. One day, when Mum's friend, Sheila, was with Mum and Adam in the bedroom, Tania listened to what they were saying and she heard Sheila saying, "You must be pleased to have a boy at last."

"Yes, of course I am," said Mum.

"Isn't your husband thrilled? Men always want sons," Sheila said.

"Didn't Dad want me?" Tania wondered, and she felt more fed up than ever with noisy little Adam.

She wondered what Mum and Dad said to each other about her and the baby when she wasn't there. She might be able to find out if she could listen to them through the baby alarm. It might be rather mean, but it wouldn't exactly be spying, because she was sure they never plotted anything bad.

It wasn't any use leaving the bit that picked up the sound in Mum's and Dad's bedroom, because it was only at night, when she was asleep, that they'd be there, talking. But if she could put it in the kitchen, and the other half in her bedroom, she'd be able to hear what they talked about over supper when she was supposed to be in bed. She had always wondered what they said to each other then.

She chose a time when Mum had taken
Adam to the shops in his pram, and Dad was
working in the garden. Then she switched
over the two bits of the alarm. She plugged the
one from Mum's bedroom in the kitchen to
receive sound and the other in her own
bedroom. She propped her giant panda up
against the alarm to hide it. Back in Mum's
room, she moved a chair so that the empty
socket didn't show.

That evening, after Mum had said goodnight, Tania crept out of bed and lay down on the floor next to the baby alarm to listen. At first she only heard Mum's footsteps. Then she heard Mum call out, "Supper's ready!" and she heard Dad say, "Coming!" She heard the screeching of chairs being drawn up to the table and the clatter of knives and forks on plates.

Sure enough, Mum and Dad were talking, but it wasn't interesting. Mum talked a lot about the baby, and what the nurse at the clinic had said, and Dad was just saying "Yes" and "No" and getting on with eating.

Tania was getting sleepy, her eyes didn't want to stay open, and once her head fell forward with a lollop on to her chest, when suddenly she was wide awake. She had heard her own name.

"It's Tania's birthday next month. What shall we give her?" Dad was asking.

"Maybe we should try to find her a dolls' house. Susie up the road has got one," Mum said.

"Is that what Tania really wants? She doesn't play with dolls much," Dad said.

"That's right. I expect she'd rather have a train set."

"Or a bicycle."

"Bicycles cost a lot," Mum said.

"I might be able to get a second-hand one. I'll ask around at work," Dad said.

This was worth listening for, but the rest of the conversation was terribly boring. Tania went to bed and dreamed that she had a new bicycle, bright red, with shiny handlebars.

A few days later, at breakfast, Mum said, "Tania, do you mind if you don't have a birthday party this year? I'm so rushed with having the baby to look after, I don't think I can manage it."

Tania didn't mind. She was never sure that she enjoyed parties, anyway. She said, "I don't mind about the party, Mum. Especially if I can have the bike."

She saw her Mum and Dad look at each
other. Then Dad said, "Who ever said you
might get a bike?"

Tania remembered how she'd heard about
the bike and she said quickly, "No one said.
I just thought."

"Don't think too much. You might be
disappointed," Mum said.

"I'll have to be careful," Tania thought.

But it was difficult to remember what she'd heard through her spying and what she was supposed to know.

Chapter 3

One evening when she was listening in to the
baby alarm, she heard her Dad say, "I've asked
my Uncle Ned to come over this weekend.
He's going home to Ireland soon, and I'd like
him to see you and the children before he
leaves."

Mum said, "Is that your mother's brother that she calls the Pirate?"

"That's him. Too clever for his own good, he was. He's settled down now, but I believe when he was younger he was up to all sorts of tricks."

"I was thinking of the kind of pirate who wears a red spotted handkerchief round his

head and has a black patch over one eye. What is he like really?" Mum said.

"Shan't tell you. Wait and see. But don't be surprised when you see his wooden leg. Oh yes . . . and he hasn't got a black patch, but one of his eyes isn't real. It's made of glass," Dad said.

Tania didn't understand why they both laughed so much. It wasn't funny having to walk with a wooden leg instead of a real one. Or to have a glass eye. But knowing these things about Uncle Ned made her want to see him a lot.

Sunday came. Mum cooked a specially good dinner, which smelled wonderful. Dad went to the station in the car to meet his Uncle, and Tania hung around in the front garden so that she could be the first to see them. It was a bit disappointing that Uncle Ned was wearing trousers, so she couldn't see the wooden leg, and though she looked as hard as she dared, she couldn't make out which of his eyes was the glass one.

He managed very well, she thought. He walked as straight as Dad. But then Dad had said he was clever.

Tania couldn't take her eyes off him. Suddenly, he said, "Why do you look at me all the time like that? Something wrong?"

"It's rude to stare," Mum said.

"I didn't mean to be rude. I just wanted to know . . ." Tania began.

"Go on."

"I wanted to know, which leg is it?" Tania said.

"Which leg is what?" Uncle Ned asked.

"Which is the wooden one?"

"Who said I had a wooden leg?"

Tania was disappointed. "Haven't you got a glass eye either?" she asked.

"Sshhh," Tania's Dad said, and her Mum put a hand over Tania's mouth, so that she couldn't talk any more.

"Tania's a great one for talking nonsense," Dad said, and went on in a hurry to ask his uncle something about his journey home. Tania saw the uncle looking at her strangely as if he didn't understand what she'd meant.

After Uncle Ned had left, Dad asked Tania, "What made you think my uncle had a wooden leg?"

"I nearly laughed right out when you said that about a glass eye," Mum said.

Tania said, "You said he had a wooden leg and a glass eye, Dad."

"Who, me? No, I never," Dad said. He must have forgotten what he'd told Mum, Tania thought. But she couldn't explain that she'd heard him say it when she'd been listening to the baby alarm.

"I'll have to be very very careful," Tania thought.

Chapter 4

A day or two later, when she was listening to Mum and Dad talking over their supper, she heard Dad say, "I'm putting in for that job that Georgie had. It would mean more money, if I get it." Then Mum said, "When will you know about it?" and Dad said, "Should hear tomorrow or the next day."

It was the next day, at breakfast, that Tania had a fright. She heard Mum say to Dad, "I don't think the baby alarm is working properly. Adam was crying yesterday morning, and I could hardly hear him on the alarm."

"I'll have a look at it some time," Dad said.

But when he came home that evening, he'd forgotten all about the alarm. He came hurrying in and he gave Mum a big hug. "Good news!" he said, and Tania forgot again and asked, "Did you get Georgie's job, Dad?"

Dad said, "Yes, I did," before he remembered that Tania shouldn't have known anything about it.

He said, "Hey, how do you know about the job? I never told you."

Tania said, "I don't know. I just sort of thought you might."

"That's funny," Dad said, and he looked at Tania at if he couldn't understand what was going on.

Tania kept very quiet after that. She didn't want Dad to discover what she'd been doing. But the evening before her birthday, she was too excited to sleep, so after Mum had said goodnight, she got out of bed and crouched down on the floor beside the baby alarm to listen to what Mum and Dad were saying to each other.

She heard Dad say, "I've put the bike in the garden shed and locked the door. I'll get it out first thing tomorrow, before I have to go off to work."

"She'll be really pleased," Mum was saying.

"It was a bit of luck Edie wanting to sell her boy's bike just now."

"Strange that Tania was talking about getting a bike," Mum said.

"Funny that she guessed about the job, too. I hope she's not going to be one of those whizz kids who can tell what's going to happen tomorrow," Dad said.

"Tania isn't like that. She's just a nice, ordinary kid," Mum said.

"She's not ordinary! Tania's my very special girl!" Dad said.

"Yes, she is. We'll be lucky if this baby turns out half as good," Mum said.

When Tania heard that she was really pleased. Ever since Adam had been born, she'd wondered whether Mum and Dad really liked her as much as they did him. But now that she'd heard them say she was special, she felt happy.

She climbed into bed, smiling all over her face. Everything was fine. It would be her birthday tomorrow and she was going to get a bike. She thought she'd put the baby alarm back the right way round tomorrow, and Mum and Dad would never find out how it was that she knew things they hadn't told her.

Just before she fell asleep, she had another thought, and this was that perhaps, if people had to have babies, Adam wasn't so bad, after all.

Anne Forsyth

Mandy's Mermaid

Illustrated by *Thelma Lambert*

Chapter One

"Oh, Mandy," said the teacher. "You
haven't been listening." Mandy blinked.
She'd been miles away, drifting through an
enchanted wood, making up a story about a
fairy-tale princess and a magic web.

Mandy sighed and left the enchanted
wood. But she soon became really
interested in what the teacher was saying.

This term the class was doing a project on the seashore. They would write about the shore, and draw pictures of their finds, and make a collage. Mandy got quite excited. Who knows what we might find, she thought.

Next day the class set out for the shore. The children made their way down the narrow street from school, past the harbour – which was empty today because all the fishing boats were out at sea.

They set off along the sand towards the rocks.

Some children began collecting shells and
seaweed. Some were watching for terns and
oyster catchers and other sea birds. Others
were looking in the rock pools for mussels
and barnacles. Everyone was busy except
Mandy who was dreaming as usual.

She began to scramble over the rocks. "Don't go too far," said the teacher.

Mandy knew that when the tide was out there was a little sandy spot with large rocks. She had almost reached the rocks when she heard a strange sound – a sort of wailing. There was something – or someone – behind the largest rock.

She craned over to see what was making the noise.

To her surprise, it was a girl – a girl with long, straight fair hair. She was sitting on a rock, swaying backwards and forwards and crooning. Mandy moved nearer.

The girl's hair hung down to her waist, and below. Mandy stared. The girl wasn't wearing anything at all, except a long fishy tail.

Mandy gazed. Then she said out loud, "It's a mermaid!" She couldn't believe her luck.

"Oh," said the girl, startled. "You did give me a fright."

"Sorry," Mandy muttered, still staring.

"I thought it would be quiet here," said the mermaid in a whining sort of voice. "But there's hordes of people."

"It's our class," said Mandy. She couldn't stop looking at that long tail all sparkling with fish scales.

"We're doing a project," she added (though in fact Mandy had done very little towards the project).

"Where did you come from?" she asked, becoming a little bolder.

"From the sea, of course," said the mermaid.

"Oh, yes," said Mandy, very humbly.

"If you must know," the mermaid yawned, "I had a row with Mum. I said I was sick of whelks, and she said I was always grumbling and why didn't I clear up my room and . . ."

"Your room?" Mandy gaped.

"Well, my bit of the cave. It's curtained off with seaweed. She went on and on about it being cluttered with shells . . ."

Mandy was rather disappointed. She didn't think mermaids had mothers who made them tidy up their rooms. And mermaids in stories were beautiful. This one certainly had a fishy tail and fair hair but she scowled a lot and had a whiny voice.

Then the teacher, who was keeping a sharp eye on the children to make sure that no one wandered off or got into trouble, called, "Mandy!"

"Wait there," said Mandy to the mermaid, and she went scrambling back over the rocks.

By this time the other children had found shells and seaweed and interesting sea creatures. They would take the shells and seaweed, but not living things, back to the classroom.

"I've got some shells, all different," said Emily.

"I found a star fish," said Paul. Some had found limpets and barnacles and razor shells. Others had found different kinds of seaweed.

"I found a mermaid," said Mandy.

"Oh, Mandy, really!" said the teacher.

"Honestly," said Mandy. "Just behind that rock. Come on, look!"

The teacher smiled. "All right then." She followed Mandy and so did the other children.

"Listen!" said Mandy. "You can hear her singing. She's just behind that big rock."

And with that, there was a splash. They couldn't see anything but a ripple on the water.

"Oh, Mandy," said the teacher. "You do make up stories. It was just a fish. Come on, everyone, time we went back."

Mandy was very cross. All right, she made up stories, but this one was true.

Chapter Two

Next day was Saturday. After lunch, Mum
said, "The dog needs a good walk and I
can't take him today." Topper, the dog, sat
with his head on one side.

"All right," said Sara, Mandy's big sister.
"I'll take him on the shore. Coming,
Mandy?"

Mandy and her family – Mum, Dad, and Sara (and Topper) – lived in an old stone house overlooking the shore. Mandy liked to look out over the waves. "Just imagine," she thought, "maybe there's a palace under the sea. And they have great feasts served by dolphins on cockleshells."

"Really, Mandy," Mum sometimes said a little crossly, "you're always day-dreaming."

That Saturday afternoon, Mandy and
Sara set off for the shore, with Topper on
his lead. Topper liked splashing in the sea
and chasing sticks, so Sara took off his lead
and they were soon racing across the sands.
Mandy followed slowly.

Then she heard the singing. She
scrambled over the rocks, and there was the
mermaid, combing her hair and humming
tunelessly.

"You shouldn't have gone off like that," said Mandy. "No one believed me."

"Hard luck," said the mermaid. "I went home," she added. "I didn't want to miss my tea." She said pathetically, "I don't suppose you've got anything to eat, have you?"

Mandy felt in her pocket. "I've got a packet of crisps. Prawn flavour."

"Mmm . . ." The mermaid ripped open the packet and began crunching. "Yummy . . ."

"What's it like under the sea?" Mandy was longing to know.

The mermaid yawned. "Nothing but caves and seaweed and no one to talk to. Fish are the dullest creatures – and they're scared of us mermaids anyway. There are seals sometimes – and dolphins, but they're boring too."

"But what about parties and feasts? I thought there might be a sea palace," said Mandy a little desperately. She was beginning to be disappointed in the mermaid.

"Well, the Bass Rock mermaids are giving a party next week – but they're such a snooty lot. I wish I had a new brush and comb, and looked – well, different," said the mermaid.

"My sister has a special brush," said Mandy. "She wouldn't mind if you borrowed it."

The mermaid brightened up.

"And – er – what do you call it? Make-up?" said the mermaid. "I've seen people on the sands wearing paint on their faces and red on their lips."

"Lipstick," said Mandy. "I'll see what I can find."

"Great," said the mermaid, not adding "thank you". She seemed rather rude, thought Mandy, but then you couldn't expect mermaids to be like ordinary people.

"Another thing," said Mandy, "why do you always sing that wailing song, if you don't mind me asking?"

"It's the only one I know," said the mermaid, sulking again.

"I know lots of good songs," said Mandy. "Pop songs. I'll teach you another, if you like."

"Don't mind," said the mermaid.

"There's a mermaid on the rocks," said
Mandy, when she caught up with Sara.
"With a long fishy tail," she added. "She'd
like to borrow your styling brush and
make-up."

"You do talk a lot of rubbish," said Sara.
"Come on, Topper, time to go home."

Chapter Three

"Well, I *did* ask," said Mandy next day as she borrowed Sara's brush and make-up, and popped them into a bag.

When next Mandy and Mum went out with the dog, Mandy climbed over the rocks. The mermaid was there, waiting. Mandy brought the bag out of her pocket.

"Mmm . . ." said the mermaid, as she opened it. "What's this?"

"Blusher," said Mandy crossly. "You put it on your cheeks to give you colour." The mermaid didn't seem at all grateful. And Sara would probably be very annoyed when she found some of her make-up had vanished.

A few days later, Mandy hardly knew the mermaid. Her straight fringe was curled and she had made up her face.

But she still complained. "After the Bass Rock party, there won't be any other parties for ages. Life's so dull."

Mandy was beginning to be sorry she had been kind to this bad-tempered creature. Then she had an idea.

"You could come to the Gala."

"What's that?" The mermaid yawned again.

"It's every year," said Mandy. "It's for the schools – well, for everyone, really. There's a procession and we decorate the lorries. Our school's doing a lorry about the seashore with sand and fishing nets . . ." Her voice trailed off.

Suddenly she had had a brainwave.

"You could be on our lorry! It's called a float, actually," she explained.

"No," said the mermaid.

"Please!" said Mandy. "We all dress up. It'll be fun."

"No way," said the mermaid and dived beneath the waves.

Mandy followed Mum and Topper home, very cross indeed. "I'm finished with her," she said.

But a few days later, gathering shells with Sara, she heard a strange sound – like someone singing.

She knew right away it was one of the pop songs she had taught the mermaid.

"Hello," said the mermaid, as Mandy climbed over the rocks. "I've thought about it. I'll be on your float. But I don't want people laughing at me because I'm a mermaid. I want to look beautiful. I want to dress up."

Mandy had never heard anyone say "I want" quite so often. She sighed. "OK. I'll see what I can do."

On the way home Mandy thought about it. Then she knew exactly what she needed. It was in the dressing-up box at school, and it hadn't been used since the pantomime last Christmas. She was sure the teacher wouldn't mind.

"What do you want it for?" asked the teacher.

"It's for a friend to wear in the Gala," said Mandy.

"Well, come along and we'll see if it's still there." She delved into the box, and there it was, wrapped in tissue paper.

"Oh, thank you," Mandy beamed. "I'll take great care of it."

That day Mandy could hardly wait to see the mermaid. Surely this would make her smile.

"I've brought you something to wear in the procession," said Mandy.

"Wow!" said the mermaid, and her face broke into a smile. "Diamonds!"

"Well," said Mandy, "Not real diamonds. But it's a tiara."

The mermaid tried it on, and admired her reflection in a pool. "Mmm . . ." she said. "I don't mind being in your procession."

Actually, Mandy knew that the mermaid was longing to be in the procession, especially now that she had the tiara to wear. Because there was nothing the mermaid enjoyed quite as much as showing off.

"Right," said Mandy. "But I wonder how I can get you on to the float. The floats will be parked on the front, near the harbour. Could you manage to get on to the quay? I'll help you."

"I'll manage," said the mermaid. "But I can't be out of the water too long. You'll need buckets of water, so that I don't get too dry."

"I'll do what I can," promised Mandy.

"Come on, Mandy," called Mum. "What *are* you doing?"

At home, Mandy found two plastic buckets. She would fill them at the tap down by the harbour. If she kept refilling the buckets – and surely her friend Lisa would help – they could keep the mermaid wet. It wasn't far from the harbour up to the Town Hall where the procession ended.

She was quite proud of herself for thinking of this. "Use your common sense," Mum kept saying. Well, this time she had.

Chapter Four

Mandy's class had gone to a lot of trouble
to decorate the float. They had a lobster
creel and fishing nets, and buckets of shells,
and seaweed. One girl was a fishwife, in a
striped skirt and shawl. Some boys were
fishermen, pretending to draw in the nets.
Mandy was to be in the middle, pretending
to build a sandcastle.

When Mandy arrived at half-past one, with her buckets, there were lots of people around. "Listen," she said to Lisa, "would you help . . .?" And then to her astonishment, she saw the mermaid already on the float. She was sitting on a fish box and she was wearing the tiara, slightly askew. She had curled her fringe and was wearing make-up.

"I got here on my own," she said. "But I'm so cold." Mandy did hope she wasn't going to sulk.

"Look," she said, "have my anorak."

"Who on earth's that?" said Mandy's teacher.

"A friend of mine," said Mandy. "She's a
–" she nearly said "a mermaid", then
changed it to "dressed up as a mermaid."

"Who's that?" asked another teacher.

"A friend of Mandy's."

"Must be from the Secondary."

"Well, I suppose it's all right. She's gone
to such trouble with her costume. Really
splendid."

"Look," said a very young child. "A fish."

"Don' t be silly," said his big sister. "It's a mermaid, but not a real one. You never saw a mermaid wearing an anorak. It's just someone dressed up."

The parade moved off, led by the Gala Queen and her attendants in a vintage car.

The mermaid took off her anorak and began combing her hair.

And then it began to rain, a few drops at first, then it became a steady drizzle. People put up umbrellas and huddled under plastic capes. But the mermaid was delighted. She was all wet, just as wet as if she'd been in the sea. Mandy was pleased too – now there was no need to run backwards and forwards with buckets of water. And the mermaid was smiling!

All the way until the procession stopped in front of the town hall, she waved and smiled.

"Isn't she great! What a good costume!" people said.

When the judges reached Mandy's float, they immediately handed a first-prize ticket to the teacher in charge. Second were the pirates from another school who had been singing "Yo, ho, ho" all the way and were quite hoarse by now.

Chapter five

After all that, the children got down from
the floats and went off to see the old fire
engines or watch the Highland dancers.
The mermaid sat on the lorry, still smiling.
And it rained and rained.

From time to time, Mandy came back to
bring her a packet of crisps or a choc ice.
Soon the mermaid had chocolate all round
her mouth and her tiara had slipped.

Half way through the
afternoon, the children
queued up for bags of
food – each one got a
paper bag with a bun
and a cake and a biscuit,
and a carton of juice.

"Can I have two bags,
please?" asked Mandy.

"Sorry, only one each," said the
teacher who was giving them out.

"It's for my friend."

"Tell her to come along herself."

The teacher turned to another member of
the staff. "You do have to watch. There's
always someone tries to get two bags . . ."

So Mandy went back to the mermaid and they shared the bag of food and the carton of juice.

Then Mandy went off to watch the tug of war. A little later, she thought she'd better see how the mermaid was getting on. It was still raining, but she would probably be happier back in the sea. But to Mandy's horror, the floats had gone.

"Where's our lorry?" Mandy asked a boy who was sucking an ice lolly nearby.

"Gone back to the harbour."

"Come on!" said Mandy to Lisa. "I must find out what's happened to her."

"Happened to who?" said Lisa, rather puzzled.

"The mermaid, of course," said Mandy.

"But I thought . . ." said Lisa.   Surely it hadn't been a *real* mermaid?

"Come *on*!" said Mandy.

They ran all the way from the town park down to the harbour. There was the lorry with its fishing nets and buckets and shells. The drivers had left the floats and gone off for a cup of tea.

And there on the box where the mermaid had sat, was the tiara.

Later, the children were helping to clear the float.

"The mermaid looked splendid," said the teacher. "What happened to your friend, Mandy? And who was she?"

"Er . . ." said Mandy, because she didn't really know what had happened.

Mandy never saw the mermaid again. But deep down under the sea, the mermaid was telling everyone about her adventures.

She made a special trip to tell the Bass Rock mermaids.

In time, the sea creatures became rather tired of hearing the story.

"I bet she made it all up," said one.

"Fancy being in a parade," said another.

"Well, I don't believe a word of it," said a passing seal. "A fishy tale, if you ask me."

But the mermaid just smiled.

Mandy thought about the mermaid sometimes. And one summer evening, when it was light long after bedtime, the family went for a walk along the shore.

Suddenly, over the waves, you could hear a voice singing a pop song.

"People with radios," said Mum, "shouldn't be allowed."

"Tuneless rubbish," said Dad, who liked Scottish fiddle music.

"I can sing better than that," said Sara.

Topper raised his head and howled.

But Mandy didn't say anything. She knew just who was singing.

Penelope Lively

Princess by Mistake

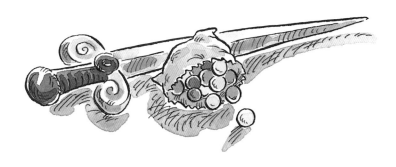

Illustrated by Julie Anderson

Chapter One

A long time ago, when I was young, on a Wednesday afternoon, a very strange thing happened to me. So strange, you probably won't believe it.

I know it was a Wednesday, because we always went to the library on Wednesday afternoons, my mother and my sister Sally and I.

And all the way home
from the library my sister Sally
and I had a fight. Sally said
I'd got a stupid lot of books –
they were all about aeroplanes
which was what I was interested in
at the time – and I said the ones she
had were boring and babyish. Fairy stories, they
were. Load of old rubbish! I jeered. Kings and
queens! Fairy godmothers! Princesses! And we
went on fighting each other all around the house
till suddenly my mother had had enough and she
turned us out.

So off we wandered, up the street, arguing away about one thing and another at the tops of our voices. We argued about who could run fastest and jump highest and swim best and then we got on to each other's personal appearance. Sally passed a few remarks about my freckles and I had a go at her long fair hair, of which she was excessively proud.

"Goldilocks!" I shouted. "S'pose you think you're the queen of the fairies! S'pose you think you're a princess!"

That was unwise, because Sally was very vain about her hair. She went bright scarlet and flew at me, and we rolled into the ditch together, scuffling.

It was the ditch outside Mr Crackington-Smith's garden. Mr Crackington-Smith was an elderly bachelor with a reputation for being difficult. He kept himself to himself and had awkward relations with his neighbours. Sally and I were so busy with our fight that neither of us saw him watching us over his gate, nor heard him say, "Will you kindly stop making that unpleasant noise outside my house."

Presently, though, we stopped for a breather and looked up and saw him scowling at us. He said, "Go away!"

And we sat there, all muddy and red in the face, and Sally said, very quietly, so quietly you wouldn't have thought he could possibly have heard, "Why should we?"

Mr Crackington-Smith said, "Because I'm telling you to. And if you don't," he went on, with a positive gleam in his eye, "I shall remove you."

We stared. Mr Crackington-Smith was quite a small man; we were rather large children. We heaved ourselves out of the ditch in silence, and shuffled about at the edge of the road. In fact we were just about to go, but Sally couldn't resist saying – to me, rudely, in a half-whisper – "I s'pose he thinks he's a magician or something?"

Mr Crackington-Smith took a pair of secateurs out of his pocket and started doing something to a rose. "As a matter of fact I am," he said calmly.

I sniggered.

Which was one of the stupidest things I ever did.

Chapter Two

After that everything happened at once. There was a great crack of thunder, and a flash of lightning. For exactly half a minute it rained very small toads; a number of black cats appeared on the garden wall and squalled horribly; broomsticks clattered around us like autumn leaves, and there was a loud thud of horse's hooves.

Sally gave a kind of squeak,
and I looked round to see her
being heaved, kicking and struggling,
on to the back of an enormous
black horse by a huge figure
in full armour wearing a crown.
"Help!" she bellowed.

I just had time to see, as the person arranged
her across the saddle in front of him, thrashing
about like a fish in a net, that she was done up in
full fairy-story princess gear – long frock, flowers in
her hair, the lot – and then the person dug his
spurs into the horse and away they went down the
road, sparks flying from the tarmac, Sally yelling
blue murder.

"Well," said Mr Crackington-Smith smugly, "satisfied?"

I said faintly: "What's he going to do with her?"

Mr Crackington-Smith was busy with his pruning now. "Oh, the usual stuff, I expect," he said. "Impenetrable dungeon with rats and snakes and all that. Standard fate of princesses. You'd better get on with it, hadn't you?"

"Get on with what?"

"Rescuing her, you stupid boy," said Mr Crackington-Smith irritably. He glanced at me and added, "I suppose we'd better give you a bit of the normal equipment."

There was a hiss and a clunk, and I found a very large heavy sword stuck firmly into my belt.

"Well," said Mr Crackington-Smith, "all the best." He put the secateurs in his pocket and began to walk towards his house.

I said desperately, "What do I *do*?"

Mr Crackington-Smith looked over his shoulder. "Oh, for goodness' sake!" he said. "Just the straightforward routine! Impossible tasks; dragons and ogres and whatnot; spells; everybody else having an unfair advantage. Just do your best. The sword's a bit blunt, by the way. Oh, and I daresay you might find these come in handy too."

I felt something in my hands and looked down to find myself holding, in one, a packet of gobstoppers and in the other a folded-up comic. "How do I *start*?" I yelled.

His voice floated back through the closing front-door. "The Blue Star Garage, of course. He'll be turning that clapped-out old nag into a car by now. You'll know which by the usual signs."

The door slammed.

I set off down the road, the sword banging uncomfortably against my leg with every step. I passed one or two people I knew, but nobody gave me a second look: whatever was happening was happening only to Sally and me. The sword slapped my leg and glittered in the sunshine.

Chapter Three

I reached the garage. There were several cars being filled up with petrol, and a red van. The van-driver had his back to me, but the van had large black letters on it that said CASTLE DESPAIR PEST CONTROL SERVICE TEL. DRAGONSWICK 469. There was a sound of banging and shouting from inside the closed doors.

The driver turned to look at me, with an evil grin; I saw the glint of chain mail under his overalls. He got into the van, slammed the door, and drove off at high speed.

I stood there, staring after it.

"Gracious me!" said a voice. "Don't just stand there, boy. Get on and *do* something."

I looked round. There was no one about, but on top of one of the petrol pumps was a small green frog. Which, you must admit, is not at all the place you'd expect to find a small green frog. It all fitted.

I said to it, "How?"

"Put me in your pocket," said the frog. "I can see you're an amateur – you'll never cope with this on your own. Ouch! Don't squeeze! Now – we need transport. Hop on that motorbike."

"But I don't know how to ride it," I protested, "and anyway, I'm not old enough . . ."

"Oh, don't quibble," said the frog impatiently.

I got on to the bike – it was one of those great big fast Japanese ones – and it won't surprise you to hear, I imagine, that it went off just like that, obedient as a horse. I didn't have to ride it – it just went.

We roared down the road, and just round the first bend we caught sight of the tail of the red van disappearing over the top of the hill.

"There he goes!" said the frog. "Step it up a bit!"

I said, breathlessly, as the motorbike hurtled up to seventy miles an hour, "Who is he, anyway?"

"Gracious," said the frog, "how ignorant can you get? He's the Black King, isn't he? The fear and dread of all. Stops at nothing. Every crime in the book. Collects princesses. Got twenty-nine of them locked up at his place. Your sister's a princess, I take it?"

"No," I said, "she's Sally Smithers of 14 Winterton Road."

"Ah," said the frog with interest, "case of mistaken identity, then. Must be the hair that did it. He wouldn't stop to find out, anyway. Whoa there! They went thataway . . ."

Chapter Four

We screamed round another bend and suddenly, where there ought to have been the rather ordinary view of the outskirts of the next town, with rows of semis and a few shops and a school and that kind of thing, there was a great sweep of pine forest, with mountains behind and, bang in the middle, a huge castle straight off a pantomime back-cloth – all towers and turrets and slit windows and drawbridges and what-have-you. The red van was just whisking over a drawbridge and in at the gate.

We dashed after it, and as we arrived a few hundred yards from the castle walls there was a convulsive heaving of the ground and out of it sprang a thick undergrowth of thorn bushes, as impassable as anything you ever saw. "Here we go," said the frog, "up to his old tricks. Well, we can scupper that one, I reckon. Where's your sword?"

"Here," I said. I brandished it around uncertainly, and, would you believe it, even as I did so the blessed thing turned into a great big mowing machine, like my dad's only three times the size, with THORNMASTER SUPREME in black letters on the handle.

"Let her go!" yelled the frog, and I tore into the brambles with the mower and in no time at all we had cleared a path right up to the castle entrance. The motorbike had vanished.

The drawbridge was still down. I hurried across it, and just as we reached the open gateway there was the most appalling roar and out leapt the largest dog you ever saw in your life, with – yes, you've guessed it – eight heads, all splayed out from a great iron collar with a tag saying BOHEMIAN SECURITY SERVICES – YOUR PROPERTY IS OUR CONCERN. I took six paces backwards. "Get down, you brute!" said the frog. "Quick – tranquillise it!"

I said, "What?" and then I remembered the
packet of gobstoppers in my pocket. I pulled them
out and hurled one at each head, and the dog
snapped them up and stood there sucking and
gulping and quick as a flash we were past it and
into the great courtyard of the castle.

I stared round in perplexity.
There were a great many entrances,
and a nasty smell of mushrooms, and
black ravens all over the place, shuffling up and
down the parapets. The frog, from my pocket said,
"I predict an ogre. Keep on your toes. Be prepared
for evasive action."

Chapter Five

I slipped through the nearest doorway. Inside, there was a kind of entrance hall, very cold and damp, and amazingly, the doors of a lift with a panel of buttons beside it saying FIRST FLOOR AND BANQUETING HALL; WEST TOWER AND BOILING-OIL CHAMBER; BEDROOMS 1–489; THRONE ROOM and, finally, DUNGEONS AND GUEST ROOMS.

"So far so good," said the frog.

I stepped forward and pressed the button marked DUNGEONS, and just as I did so there was a kind of howling from down a long dark stone passage, rather like the noise of an approaching plane, getting louder and nearer all the time.

"Thought so . . ." said the frog. "Watch out!" and there in front of us was an immense ogre, with a great head of shaggy red hair, dressed in sacking, armed with a club studded with six-inch nails. The frog whispered, "Play it cool – they're not very bright, usually."

I said politely, "Good morning."

"Wurra-wurra-wurra-hhrumph . . . HOP IT!" bellowed the ogre, advancing, and waving his club around.

I side-stepped hastily and said, "I won't disturb anyone. I was just going to pop down to the dungeons and rescue my sister."

"Wassat?" said the ogre, scratching his head. He didn't seem all that quick on the uptake.

The frog poked his nose out of my pocket and said, "No need to bother yourself with small fry like us – a fine strapping fellow like you."

"Grrr . . .!" said the ogre, flexing his muscles with ostentation. "Thirteen foot five in me socks; forty-one stone six pounds."

"Fantastic!" said the frog, nudging me. I edged towards the lift again, and pushed the button.

"Oy-oy . . ." growled the ogre. "Whaddya-think-yer-doing . . . HOP IT! SCRAM!"

"Amazing . . ." said the frog. "Thirteen foot five! Ever thought of tossing the caber? Javelin throwing? Olympic wrestling, that kind of thing?"

But it was the wrong approach. The ogre glared and began to rumble threateningly. "You think I'm some kinda dumb stoopid muscle man?" – I pressed the lift button as hard as I could – "You think I'm a bit thick or somefing? I'm a thinking man, I tell yer, I read books, I . . ."

"Absolutely," said the frog, "quite so. Obvious to anyone."

I groped in my pocket. "Here," I said. "Present for you . . ." and I flung the comic at the ogre as hard as I could.

He grabbed hold of it and a great beaming smile spread over his face. "Aaah!" he said. "Wow! Cor! Smashing!" He began to turn the pages over with his enormous fingers, and at that moment there was a whirr and a click and the lift doors slid open.

"Quick!" said the frog, and I shot into the lift and slammed my hand down on the START button. The doors slid shut again and the lift plunged down.

It stopped. The doors opened. I got out, cautiously.

Chapter Six

There was darkness, and stone walls streaming with water, and things that slithered off into the gloom, and flappings and squeakings and unpleasant smells. "Press on," said the frog, "this is the crunch. Himself will be somewhere about, I don't doubt."

I stumbled forward, calling, "Sally! Sally!" And after a minute or two, distantly, we heard a faint, answering voice. A number of faint, answering voices.

I rushed on, calling Sally's name, and the answering cries got closer and closer until at last I groped my way round a corner and there in front was a great padlocked door with an iron grille at the top, and Sally's face peering through it, shrieking, "Help! Get me out of here!"

"Move over," said the frog, "this is where I come in. Allowed one trick up your sleeve – it's all part of the game." And with that, he sprang out of my pocket, landed on the padlock, and turned himself into a small iron file which sliced through the metal quick as a flash. The padlock fell off, and the frog, looking a little sore around the mouth, reappeared poking his nose out of my pocket.

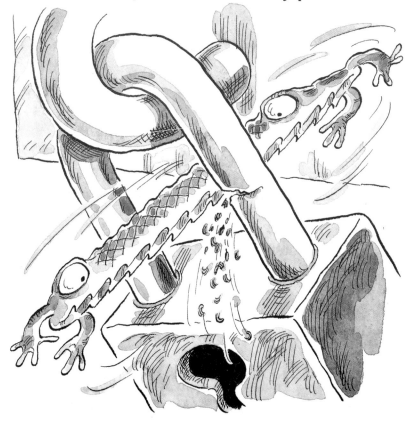

I flung the door open, and there was Sally, and
a whole lot of other girls, all weeping and wailing
and all in princess outfits. They fell on me in the
most embarrassing way. And then all of a sudden
there was a clatter of heavy footsteps in the
passage outside. "Here we go!" said the frog. "It's
up to you now! One thing – his backhand's weak."

It was the Black King. He sprang at me, armoured from top to toe, and I sprang back, with my sword in my hand (it said THORNMASTER SUPREME on the handle now – there'd been a slip-up somewhere).

We fought round and
round and up and down
and to and fro, with all the
princesses cheering like mad,
and twice I had him down and
once he had me down, and then, just
as I thought I couldn't go on a minute longer, he
gave a great howl and a banshee wail and there
was a puff of horrible black sulphurous smoke,
and he was gone.

We all streamed out of the castle, Sally and I and the princesses and the frog in my pocket. The princesses all said, "Thank you *ever* so much, that was *really* kind . . ." and went dashing off in all directions, and Sally and I leapt onto the motorbike, which had reappeared again just outside the castle, and we roared off too and . . .

Chapter Seven

There we were on the edge of the road outside
Mr Crackington-Smith's house. No motorbike, no
frog, no sword, Sally in jeans and a T-shirt again.
We looked at each other. Neither of us said
anything.

We walked home, very slowly, and we didn't say a thing but every now and then we glanced at each other, quick, and then looked away again. I knew. Sally knew. We still do. We don't talk about it, even now. It was a funny thing to happen, wasn't it – on a Wednesday afternoon. As I said, you'll have to take it or leave it, it's up to you – I'm just telling you what happened.

Catherine Robinson

MOG and BUMBLE

Illustrated by Alice Englander

For Alexander

1

Mog came to live with the Smiths a long time ago. They found him fast asleep among the packing cases and boxes when they first moved in to their house. It was snowing, and they hadn't the heart to put him out again. Then Mum gave him a saucer of milk, and that was that; he was there for good. If he'd once had another home, he never went back to it, and nobody ever came looking for him.

All this had happened such a long time ago that
Sarah couldn't remember a time when Mog wasn't
living with them.

"I can," said William. "I remember before he
came."

Sarah scoffed. "You can't! You weren't even born
then."

Sarah was Mog's little girl. They were special friends. Mog would even let Sarah tickle his tummy, which Mum said a lot of cats wouldn't put up with. And in return, Sarah would tell him what a wonderful, beautiful, extra-special cat he was.

He wasn't really.
He was just an ordinary
tabby cat with a
white bib and paws.
He was a bit battered
about the ears, because
he didn't like other cats
very much and was
always getting into
fights. And over the
last winter or two the
Smiths had noticed
him limping.

"He's got rheumatism," Dad told them. "He's
getting old." But he was still beautiful to Sarah.

One day, Mum and Dad and Sarah and William all went for a ride in the car. Mum and Dad wouldn't tell Sarah and William where they were going. They just smiled at each other from time to time.

At last, the car drew up outside a big house. Sarah could hear masses and masses of dogs, all barking at once.

"Why have we come here?" she asked Mum. "What is this place, anyway?"

"It's the RSPCA," Mum told her, still smiling. "They look after lost dogs and cats, and find homes for them."

William started to jump around with excitement. "Yah-hoo!" he shouted. He knew why they'd come. "We're getting a dog! We're getting a dog!" And Sarah could see from Mum and Dad's faces that it was true.

William had been asking for a dog for ages, but
Mum and Dad had never said anything except "We'll
see." Sarah hated it when they said that. She knew it
usually meant "No." But this time, it must have
meant "Yes." At first, Sarah didn't like the idea very
much. She wasn't sure how Mog would feel about
having a dog around the place. But when she saw
the dogs, she changed her mind.

As the Smiths walked up and down the concrete paths, trying to choose one, all the dogs came right up to the wire netting. They wagged their tails and pressed their wet noses through the holes in the fence. Some of them even jumped up and down, eager to be chosen as William's dog. Sarah would have liked to have taken them all home, but she knew they couldn't. She didn't like to think about what might happen to the dogs they didn't choose.

William finally
picked one. It was
a puppy, with soft-
looking fluffy brown
fur. One ear stood up
straight while the
other sort of flopped
over one eye. The
other eye had a white
patch around it.

"Isn't he cute?"
William yelled with
pleasure.

Dad agreed he was.
"Look at him bumbling
along; he knows he's
going home with you!"

Mum and Dad sorted things out with the RSPCA man. Then they drove home, with the new puppy on William's lap in the back of the car.

"You'll have to think of a name for him," Mum told William. "How about Patch? That's a good name."

William shook his head. "No. His name's Bumble."

Mog was waiting at the front door when the Smiths got home. He stood up and stretched when he saw them. He rubbed his head around Sarah's legs and miaowed to be let in. He didn't see William carrying Bumble.

Mum opened the front door, and William put
Bumble down on the ground. The puppy ran
straight past Mog and into the kitchen, where he
found Mog's food on the floor. He bounced over to
it and swallowed it all down with a glooping sound.
Then he stuck his nose in Mog's milk, and glooped
that down too.

Mog stared at the puppy in amazement. But the
amazement didn't last for long. He arched his back
and fluffed up his fur and puffed up his tail like a
brush, and hissed fiercely at Bumble. Bumble had
never seen a cross cat before, and thought Mog was
playing. He bumbled round him, wagging his little
tail with pleasure. Mog hissed again, and when
Bumble got too close he lifted a paw and whacked
the puppy around the ear.

Bumble yelped with fright as he rolled over and over, head over tail. He ended up in a crumpled little heap by the back door.

"Bumble!" William yelled, upset. "Naughty cat, Mog!" And he went to smack him.

But Mum stopped him. "Don't do that, William," she said. "They're going to have to get used to each other. Mog's bound to be annoyed at first."

Sarah picked Mog up to soothe him, and William picked up Bumble. But neither of them would be soothed. Mog was still fluffed up and cross. He scratched Sarah for the very first time as he wriggled and wroggled and tried to escape from her arms. And Bumble was so scared by his close encounter with this strange spitting thing that he made a puddle, all down William's shirt.

"Oh Bumble," William said sadly, as Mum led him away to be changed.

"Oh Mog," Sarah whispered, as she sucked her scratched hand. She knew it had been an accident, but it still hurt. But the hurt was more inside her than on her hand. She wondered if Mog and Bumble would ever get used to each other, as Mum had said. It hadn't been a very good start.

4

It didn't carry on very well, either. For weeks, whenever the puppy appeared, bumbling innocently along, Mog would hiss and cuff Bumble around the ear. So Mum gave them beds in separate rooms; Bumble in the kitchen, and Mog in luxury on the spare room bed.

"That cat is spoilt," Dad grumbled.

"He's upset," Sarah said firmly, burying her face in Mog's purring silky side. "He has to get used to Bumble."

"Bumble has to get used to Mog, too," William said. "He keeps bashing him. Why does he keep bashing him, Mummy?"

But Mum had no real answer.

Mog soon grew tired of bashing Bumble. He
started hiding behind doors instead and then leaping
out at the puppy, doubled in size and hissing and
spitting like a whole Bonfire Night of fireworks.
Bumble soon stopped trotting happily along. He
began to look nervously about him as he went. The
whole family was getting fed up with Mog disturbing
the household.

"That cat's a menace," Dad grumbled. Privately, Sarah was beginning to agree with him. But she would never tell that to Mog.

Bumble was a bit of a menace, too. He kept digging up the plants in the garden and eating them. And he didn't understand that he was supposed to go outside to do his puddles and things. Mum was getting very fed up with cleaning them up off the carpet.

"They're *both* menaces," she grumbled one day. She was on her hands and knees yet again with a bucket of hot water, strong with disinfectant. "I can't stand much more of this. One of them will have to go."

Nobody thought she really meant it, not even Mum. She was just cross at forever having to clean up Bumble's messes and cope with Mog's fireworks. But later on, Sarah remembered Mum's words, and wondered if Mog had overheard.

It was a lovely bright sunny Sunday, and Dad
decided they would all take Bumble for a
walk.

"We'll go to the park," he declared. "Get some
fresh air. And we can teach Bumble to fetch
sticks."

Mum laughed, and called Dad an optimist. Sarah
didn't know what that meant, but they both sounded
happy. It was the first time Mum had laughed like
that since Bumble had come to live with them.

So off they went. Dad had Bumble on his new
lead. Sarah was wearing her Christmas present scarf
and gloves, and William had on his new shiny red
wellington boots, which he kept stopping to admire.

Suddenly, Sarah realised that Mog was following
them. He'd never done that before; he didn't usually
want to be anywhere near Bumble.

"Go home, Mog!" she told him. And then, more crossly, "Go home! You can't come to the park with us – go home!"

But still Mog followed them, trailing behind and hiding in bushes, and then running fast to catch them up. Sarah was worried because they had to cross a main road to get to the park. Cars and buses and lorries whizzed along it, and she knew that Mog didn't realise you were supposed to use the zebra crossing to get to the other side. She didn't even think Mog knew what zebra crossings were. She had once seen him sit down in the middle of their road to

have a little wash, and not move out of the way even when a car came. The driver had to get out of the car and pick Mog up. He set him down on the side of the road, and Mog had continued with his wash, quite unbothered.

"Make him go home, Mum," Sarah said, concerned.

But Mum told her to ignore him. "He'll soon go home by himself," she said. And she seemed to be right. Mog stayed on the right side of the busy main road, and when they finished their walk in the park and came back, there was no sign of him.

6

That afternoon, Sarah went to play at her friend Sophie's house. When she got back home, she felt that something wasn't quite right. But it wasn't until supper time that she realised what it was.

"Where's Mog?" she asked Mum. "Have you seen him?"

"Why, no," Mum replied. "Now you come to mention it. Let me put his supper down; that'll soon make him appear."

But it didn't. And he hadn't appeared by the time William went to bed, or at Sarah's bedtime either.

When William was very little he had once lost Albert, his teddy. He had cried for three days until Albert turned up at the back of the airing cupboard, where he had pushed him and then forgotten about him.

Now Sarah knew
how he had felt. She
wandered around the
house with a lump in
her throat, calling
Mog, although she
knew he wasn't there
and couldn't hear her.
She even made Mum
look in the airing
cupboard, remembering
Albert. But Mog wasn't
there.

Dad went into the garden with a torch, and looked in the shed and the garage, but Mog wasn't there either. Then Dad put his coat on and walked up to the main road by the park. Sarah knew where he had gone, although nobody told her. She imagined Mog's furry tabby body squashed in a sad heap on the road.

But when Dad came back he didn't have Mog with him, squashed or otherwise. He shook his head.

"I'm sorry, Sarah," he said softly. "There's no sign of him."

Mum bustled around her and took her up to bed. She made her some cocoa. She even read her a story and tucked her in with a kiss, like she used to, when Sarah was younger.

"Cheer up, sweetheart," she said gently, stroking the hair from Sarah's forehead. "Mog will be all right. He's a wise old cat. He can look after himself, just you wait and see."

But Sarah didn't believe her. She lay in bed once Mum had turned the light off, with tears rolling down her face and a nasty tight feeling in her throat. All she could hear were Mum's words; "One of them will have to go."

7

Sarah woke up very early the next morning. It was so early it was still dark. For a moment she just lay there, half asleep. Then she remembered; Mog.

She fell out of bed and stumbled down the stairs, and opened the front door. The street lamp lit up the road with a ghostly orange glow. There was nobody about; no cars, no people. No Mog.

"Mog!" she called, in a whisper. "Oh, Mog! Where are you?"

But he didn't come running to her.

Sarah shivered on the doorstep. She closed the door and went back upstairs, although she didn't want to. She got back into bed and lay awake for ages, thrashing around and thinking terrible thoughts about poor lost Mog. At last she fell asleep.

She was woken again when it was properly morning, by the sound of Mum going downstairs. Sarah ran down the stairs after her.

"Mum," she called, but quietly. She didn't want to wake Dad and William. "Do you think . . ."

Then she stopped. Mum had opened the door to bring the milk in; and there, on the doorstep next to the three pints, sat Mog! He ran in, miaowing.

Sarah gasped with happiness. She couldn't speak. She just picked him up and cuddled him and kissed him. Mum kissed Sarah, and smiled at them both.

"You see," she said, later on. "I knew he'd come back!"

"So did I," said Sarah. "So did I, really."

"Where do you think he's been?" William wanted
to know at breakfast. "What's he been doing? Where
did he sleep?"

"He's had a night on the tiles, that's all," Dad said.
"No harm done. He knows home's the best place to
be."

Sarah thought a night on the tiles sounded
uncomfortable. She got Mum to open a tin of tuna
as a special breakfast for Mog.

"That cat's a glutton," said Dad. But he looked
pleased Mog was back, all the same.

174

Everyone was pleased to see Mog; even Bumble, who wagged his tail happily when Sarah put Mog down. Sarah and William thought they might be friends now. But Mog puffed up in his usual way, and would have bashed Bumble if Sarah hadn't hastily picked him up to give him another 'welcome home' cuddle. She had thought he'd run away because he hated Bumble, and didn't want to live with the Smiths any more. But now he was back. To Sarah, that was all that mattered.

Later that afternoon, Bumble was out in the garden.
He had his lead on, and it was attached to the
washing line. Dad had discovered that he could still
run around like that, but he couldn't get at the plants
and eat them.

All of a sudden, there was a tremendous woofing
from the garden; "I thought it was a billion dogs,"
Sarah said afterwards.

"I thought it was a trillion," said William, not to be
outdone.

In actual fact, it was only two dogs; but they were very big. They had jumped over the fence at the bottom of the garden and were barking fiercely at poor Bumble, who was still tied to the washing line. He was a little shivering heap on the ground.

"Mummy!" yelled William, bursting into tears.

"Dad!" shrieked Sarah. "Come quickly! They're killing Bumble!"

But before Mum or Dad could do anything, a flash of tabby lightning came bursting from the rose bushes. It was Mog. He whirled around, hissing and spitting and flashing his claws.

The dogs had never seen anything like it. They were used to chasing cats, not the other way around. They fled in fright, leaping over the fence much quicker than they had leapt in.

Mum, Dad, William and Sarah all went into the garden. Dad untied Bumble, who jumped up and tried to lick everybody's face. Now the big dogs had gone, he was ready to play again.

Mog was sitting on the ground, back to his normal size. He washed his ears carefully, and ignored the puppy.

"Mog saved Bumble!" William beamed. "Isn't he brilliant!"

"Fancy standing up to those dogs like that!" Dad exclaimed. "That cat's a marvel!"

"He certainly is," agreed Mum. "Perhaps he's at last accepted Bumble's here to stay."

Sarah didn't say anything. She just picked Mog up,and buried her face in his fur. She was very proud of him.